# Smythe Gambrell Library

Given in memory of
Dr. Frank Bertalan,
father of Mrs. Joan Friedman
by
The Smythe Gambrell
Library Staff

WORLD ALMANAC® LIBRARY OF THE MIDDLE AGES

# Cities and towns

IN THE MIDDLE AGES

## MERCEDES PADRINO

WORLD ALMANAC® LIBRARY

Please visit our web site at: www.worldalmanaclibrary.com
For a free color catalog describing World Almanac® Library's list of high-quality books and multimedia programs, call 1-800-848-2928 (USA) or 1-800-387-3178 (Canada). World Almanac® Library's fax: (414) 332-3567.

Library of Congress Cataloging-in-Publication Data

Padrino, Mercedes.
    Cities and towns in the Middle Ages / by Mercedes Padrino.
        p. cm. — (World Almanac Library of the Middle Ages)
    Includes bibliographical references and index.
    ISBN 0-8368-5893-X (lib. bdg.)
    ISBN 0-8368-5902-2 (softcover)
    1. Cities and towns, Medieval—Europe—Juvenile literature.  2. Civilization, Medieval—Juvenile literature.  I. Title.  II. Series.
HT115.A45   2005
307.76'094'0902—dc22                                                2005043265

First published in 2006 by
**World Almanac® Library**
A Member of the WRC Media Family of Companies
330 West Olive Street, Suite 100
Milwaukee, WI 53212  USA

Produced by White-Thomson Publishing Ltd.
Editor: Walter Kossmann
Volume editor: Peg Goldstein
Designer: Malcolm Walker
Photo researcher: Amy Sparks
World Almanac® Library editorial direction: Valerie J. Weber
World Almanac® Library editor: Jenette Donovan Guntly
World Almanac® Library art direction: Tammy West
World Almanac® Library graphic design: Kami Koenig
World Almanac® Library production: Jessica Morris and Robert Kraus

Photo credits:
Akg-Images: pp. cover, 11,15, 33, 35 (Erich Lessing), 5, 6 (Schuetze /Rodemann), 22, 36, 40 (British Library), 16, 38, 43; Art Archive: pp. 31 (Museo Civico, Bologna/Dagli Orti ); Bridgeman Art Library: pp. title page, 9 (Bibliothéque de L'Arsenal, Paris), 4 (Bibliothéque Royale de Belgique, Brussels), 8 (Castello di Issogne, Val d'Aosta, Italy), 14, 17, 24, 32 (Osterreichische Nationalbibliothek, Vienna), 20 (Inner Temple, London), 21, 28 (Archives Charmet), 23 (Louvre, Paris/Lauros/Giraudon), 25 (Museo Correr, Venice), 26 (British Library), 27 (Bibliothéque Municipale, Castres, France/Giraudon), 30 (John Bethell), 34 (Castello di Issogne, Val d'Aosta/Giraudon), 37 (Bibliothéque Nationale, Paris/Giraudon), 41 (Fitzwilliam Museum, University of Cambridge); Corbis: pp. 12,18.

*Cover: Ambrogio Lorenzetti painted this fresco of buildings in Siena, Italy, in 1338.*
*Title page: This fifteenth-century illumination shows the streets of Paris.*

Printed in Canada

1 2 3 4 5 6 7 8 9 09 08 07 06 05

# Contents

Words that appear in the glossary are printed in **boldface** type the first time they occur in the text.

**Source References** on page 45 give bibliographic information on quoted material. See numbers ( [1] ) at the bottom of quotations for their source numbers.

# Introduction

he Middle Ages are the period between ancient and early modern times—the years from about A.D. 500 to 1500. In that time, Europe changed dramatically. The Middle Ages began with the collapse of the **Roman Empire** and with "**barbarians**" invading from the north and east. In the early years of the Middle Ages, western European farmers struggled to survive. This period ended with European merchants eagerly seeking new international markets, European travelers searching for lands and continents unknown to them to explore, European artists creating revolutionary new styles, and European thinkers developing powerful new ideas in religion, government, and philosophy.

## What Were the "Middle Ages" Like?

Some people view the period as the "Dark Ages," an era marked by ignorance and brutality. It is true that **medieval** people faced difficult lives marred by hard work, deadly diseases, and dreadful wars, but their lives included more than that.

The Middle Ages were also a time of growing population, developing technology, increasing trade, and fresh ideas. New villages and towns were built; new fields were cleared; and, with the help of new tools like the wheeled iron plow,

### A HISTORIAN'S VIEW

*"A hundred years ago the medieval centuries . . . were widely regarded as 'The Dark Ages.' . . . It was an age whose art was barbaric or 'Gothic'—a millennium of darkness—a thousand years without a bath. Today . . . scholarship [has] demonstrated clearly that the medieval period was an epoch of immense vitality and profound creativity."*
**C. Warren Hollister** [1]

farms produced more food. **Caravans** brought silks and spices from faraway lands in Asia. New sports and games, such as soccer, golf, chess, and playing cards, became popular. Musicians, singers, acrobats, and dancers entertained crowds at fairs and festivals. Traveling troupes performed plays that mixed humor with moral messages for anyone who would stop and listen.

Religion, education, and government all changed. Christianity spread throughout Europe and became more powerful. Another major faith—Islam—was born and carried into Europe from the Middle East. New schools and universities trained young men as scholars or for careers in the Church, medicine, and the law. Medieval rulers, judges, and ordinary citizens created **parliaments**, jury trials, and the common

◄ Towns were busy places that brought together large numbers of people. People are shown here buying and selling near a town gate. In towns, people not only did business but also exchanged ideas.

▲ Defense was an important concern for medieval townspeople. Carcassone, in modern-day France, was built on a hill, which was easier to defend than flat land. French kings added the walls and towers in the thirteenth century. The many high towers provided extra protection.

law. These changes in the fabric of society still shape our world today.

Historians divide the entire period into two parts. In the early Middle Ages, from about A.D. 500 to 1000, Europe adjusted to the changes caused by the fall of the Roman Empire and the formation of new kingdoms by Germanic peoples. In these years, the Christian Church took form, and Europeans withstood new invasions. In the late Middle Ages, from about 1000 to 1500, medieval life and culture matured. This period saw population growth and economic expansion, the rise of towns and universities, the building of great cathedrals and mosques, and the launching of the **Crusades**.

## Cities and Towns

Throughout the Middles Ages, Europe was mainly rural. After about 1100, though, towns and cities began to grow. Such growth had important economic, political, and social effects on the people of Europe.

Towns and cities contributed to Europe's shift from an economy based on bartering, or trading goods, to an economy based on money. The growth of towns reinforced that trend.

In the Middle Ages, many people were **serfs**. Serfs were farm laborers who lived on a **manor**, or large estate owned by a lord. Unlike free peasants, serfs were not allowed to move away from the manor. In towns, serfs could gain their freedom. It was little wonder that some serfs ran away to towns. Citizens of towns had another advantage over people who lived on manors— they did not have to pay taxes to the lord to conduct their business. Over time, towns won the right to form their own courts. This right was an early step toward self-government.

Finally, the growth of towns and cities helped make European culture more urban. Entertainment, such as street festivals and theater, was better suited to towns than to rural areas. Europe's cities also fostered universities, which brought them fame and money.

# CHAPTER 1

# the URBAN Environment

If people could go back in time to a medieval city or town, they would probably want to hold their noses. Medieval towns did not smell very nice. Animal waste sat in the streets, mingled with mud. Streets were crowded, too—narrow and full of people, carts, and animals.

## The Location of Towns

Transportation played a crucial role in the choice of a town's location. Since boats offered the fastest means of transportation in the Middle Ages, many towns arose along coasts or rivers. Even if water transportation was not a significant part of a town's economy, people needed a steady water supply for drinking and cleaning. Being nearby water, however, was a mixed blessing. Many towns were prone to flooding.

Having resources near also played a role in the location of some towns. Bordeaux, in today's France, was surrounded by a wine-producing region that contributed to the city's growth. Stockholm, in modern-day Sweden, was located in a region that produced copper, iron, and timber.

Some towns were already old in the Middle Ages. They had existed in Roman times (before

▼ Prague is located on the Vltava River in today's Czech Republic. It was founded in the ninth century where trade routes crossed. Prague quickly became a business center. By the fourteenth century, it was an important city with a cathedral and a university.

A.D. 500) and lost population over the centuries but were growing once more because of an increase in trade. Other towns arose around the main church of a **bishop**, where much of the work of the Christian Church was carried out.

Only a few cities were great business centers where merchants met to carry out international trade. Most towns served as marketplaces for their local area. Towns were located at crossroads, where country people could easily go to shop or sell their goods. **Artisans**, or craftspeople, bought local raw materials to make products, which they sold to people from the area. Local farms supplied most of the foods eaten by the townspeople: grain, meat, cheese, vegetables, fruit, beer, and wine. Only a few items, such as salt and olive oil, were brought in from more distant places.

## Town Walls

Towns across Europe were surrounded by stone and masonry walls or by fences and earthworks. These fortifications were needed for defense. Roads into and out of a town passed through gates that were closed at night to keep strangers out. During the day, gatekeepers inspected wagons coming into the towns with goods for sale. The people who brought the goods had to pay a tax on what they carried in.

Fortifications sometimes limited town growth. When a town grew too large for its existing defenses, town dwellers solved the problem by expanding the town and building a new set of defenses. Of course, people could also build upward, adding stories to existing buildings. In the thirteenth century, most medieval European towns were overcrowded, yet their populations were not large. Probably only five towns in Christian Europe had more than eighty thousand inhabitants: Paris in France; Milan, Venice, and Florence in today's Italy; and Constantinople in modern-day Turkey.

## Markets

Those who drove their carts filled with goods into towns typically did not travel far into town to begin selling. The streets just inside the town gate were often the widest, so people parked their carts and set up stalls there. Some towns had open squares that were used as marketplaces. Sometimes those squares were set amid the town's most important public buildings—the cathedral or government buildings, for instance.

Markets were noisy places: tradespeople would sing or chant about their products to attract customers, and the town crier would announce

### FAN OF LONDON

*"Among the noble cities of the world that are celebrated by Fame, the City of London, seat of the Monarchy of England, is one that spread its fame wider, sends its wealth and wares further, and lifts its head higher than all others. It is blest in the wholesomeness of its air, in its reverence for the Christian faith, in the strength of its bulwarks, the nature of its situation, the honor of its citizens, and the chastity of its matrons. It is likewise most merry in its sports and fruitful of noble men."*
**William Fitzstephen, medieval biographer, c.1180** [2]

▲ This illustration shows a busy marketplace in fifteenth-century Italy. Stalls were small and cluttered with tables and baskets filled with items for sale. In this part of the market, most shopkeepers sold fruits and vegetables.

the news of the day, perhaps calling people together with a handbell. The loud and constant sounds at times annoyed churchgoers and area residents. When they complained to the authorities, they sometimes succeeded in getting the stalls and carts moved.

### Streets and Neighborhoods

People with the same occupation tended to cluster together in medieval towns. Thus, all the potters or blacksmiths (metalworkers) would be found on the same street or in the same neighborhood. People in related occupations often settled near each other. For instance, steelmakers—who fashioned swords—lived near armorers and leather workers, who also made

military goods. With craftspeople clustered together, customers could more easily compare prices and goods among the sellers.

Medieval streets were narrow and winding. They were not laid out according to a plan. Sometimes streets were so cluttered with market stalls and display tables that people and horses could not get through.

Pollution was a problem in many areas. People dumped garbage in the street. Animal and human

### Streets of Paris

The streets of Paris were so filthy and muddy that, in 1185, King Philip Augustus ordered them to be paved. This order did not solve all the problems, however. Some streets were so narrow that only one cart could pass through at a time. Finally, in 1222, city streets were widened so that two carts could pass at the same time.

► The narrow streets of Paris had no sidewalks. Shops opened onto the streets, and artisans and merchants worked where everyone could see them. A barber (*center*) is shaving a man out in the open.

waste collected in backyards and alleys. Butchers and tanners threw animal parts and chemicals into local rivers, and the constant burning of wood and coal in shops and homes polluted the air.

## Houses

Better houses in towns were three-to-four stories high. The upper stories projected out over the street, blocking the light to the area below. Behind the houses stood storage buildings and stables. Some people planted small fruit and flower gardens behind their homes. The houses were built generally of wood, with straw roofs. The windows were made of oiled parchment, although glass came into use in the fourteenth century. Floors were covered with rushes (grassy plants). To help keep out the cold, people hung linen cloths or tapestries on the walls. Wooden houses burned easily, and houses were built close together, so spreading fire was a constant danger. People built houses of stone if it was available nearby. In many areas, though, few people could afford stone.

Typically, the merchant or artisan who owned the house operated a shop on the ground floor. Customers could look in through a window or door to see the merchandise. The second floor had a hall or a living area with a large fireplace. Next to the hall was the kitchen. It usually had a fireplace big enough for the cook to stand inside, and it shared a chimney with the hall fireplace. Family bedrooms were on the third floor, and servants' quarters were on the fourth. Most people did not live so comfortably, however. In poor neighborhoods, several families lived in one house. Poor families rented as many rooms as they could afford.

Even rich merchants had few pieces of furniture. Several family members usually shared a bed. Some wealthy people had silk bedding and feather-filled mattresses, but most people had straw mattresses with wool and linen bedding. Lice, fleas, and bedbugs were an annoyance to rich and poor alike, as were mice in the kitchen.

▶ Siena, Italy, was an important banking center in the fourteenth century. Its citizens hired great artists to beautify their city. This street scene is a small section of a large painting found in the government building which was called the Public Palace.

The wealthy sometimes had silver or gold dishes, but even they used tin and wooden dishes for everyday meals. According to one thirteenth-century writer, most households had only a table, benches, and chairs. People used cupboards and chests for storage.

## Public Buildings

The merchants and artisans who lived in urban areas took great pride in their cities and towns. They put their own time, effort, and money into constructing beautiful public spaces and buildings. Town halls, bridges, squares, and fountains were carefully designed. Public buildings were often decorated with pictures showing the town's history.

Committees of citizens frequently oversaw the construction of neighborhood churches and hired the artists who painted and sculpted the works placed in them. People did not go to church just to pray. They also went to do business. Merchants set up stalls or met to make deals in front of churches. Businesspeople often negotiated contracts in church, where people were believed to act in good faith. Town councils and guilds often held meetings in churches.

## towns and Cathedrals

Even when Church leaders, rather than the people, began a cathedral-building project, local townspeople gave it full support. Wealthy merchants made large donations, and craftspeople financed parts of the construction through their guilds. Chartres Cathedral in France, for example, had more than one hundred stained-glass windows funded by donations. Forty-four were gived by nobles, sixteen by church leaders, and forty-two by guilds.

## Islamic Cities

Arabs conquered most of Spain and Portugal in the eighth century and most of Sicily in the ninth. Their towns were laid out differently from towns in Christian areas. The mosque, or house of worship, was the heart of the city. It was used for public meetings as well as for praying. The marketplace was next to it. Market stalls were arranged by trades so that all the shoemakers or silk merchants were together. The lowliest trades—such as tanning hides—were farthest away from the mosque. Towns had public baths and gardens, and homes were separated from public areas. Different families and religious groups had their own neighborhoods. Local rulers had their palaces in or near the city. Some Muslim cities were large. Palermo, Sicily, had about 100,000 people and Córdoba, Spain, had more than 300,000.

# Social Classes and Social Roles

# Social Classes and Social Roles

People who moved into towns were mostly an ambitious group, ready to work hard and determined to succeed. They were free men and women. Most of them worked as merchants, artisans, and shopkeepers.

## The Levels of Society

Many townspeople came from a free peasant background. Some were former serfs who were no longer needed on the manors where they were born. Some were nobles without lands who went into business. Others were lawyers whose skills were needed for business and government. Christian townspeople were the main settlers looking for work and new opportunities in the border towns of Spain and central Europe. These were areas Christians conquered from Muslims and **pagan** Slavic people.

Town society was divided into groups. At the top were the **burghers**—the wealthiest and most prestigious town dwellers. Burghers were citizens of the town, generally merchants and master craftsmen who owned property there. Many had skilled employees. Burghers were actively involved in the politics of their cities and towns. Some were even given the title of **knight**. This title was given normally only to noblemen. Below the burghers were wage earners, such as artisans, and the poor.

◀ The seated man is a notary writing a document. Notaries were public officials who could write contracts and keep legal records. Burghers used a notary's services when they worked out business deals.

Urban women had the same status as their husbands and fathers. They could be involved in business, but they could not participate in politics. At all levels of society, no matter what else they did, women were supposed to obey their husbands and be dutiful mothers.

## PROPER ATTITUDE OF A YOUNG WIFE

*"You [wife], being of the age of fifteen years . . . did pray me that I would please to be indulgent to your youth and [ignorance] . . . until that you should have seen and learned more, to the hastening whereof you did promise me to set all care and diligence . . . praying me humbly . . . that for the love of God I would not correct you harshly before strangers nor before our own folk, but that I would correct you each night or from day to day in our chamber . . . and then you would not fail to amend yourself according to my teaching and correction."*
**The Goodman of Paris, *Treatise on Morals and Home Economics*, 1392** [3]

## SIR RICHARD Whittington

Richard Whittington was the son of a knight who lived on the Welsh border. He made his way to London, England, where he opened a fabric shop. Whittington amassed a great fortune and a great reputation. Over time, he became a banker, making loans to kings. Whittington was chosen lord mayor of London three times. When he died, he left his money to the poor and to his city. He was so famous that a legend arose about him. According to the story, young Dick had been a poor orphan who worked for a merchant as a kitchen servant. One day, he ran away but returned when he thought he heard the bells of London calling him back. Dick became rich by selling his pet cat to a kingdom that was overrun by mice. Eventually, he married the merchant's daughter and inherited the merchant's business.

## Merchants and Masters

Merchants engaged in commerce—buying and selling goods—rather than making products themselves. Some merchants took part in trade with distant regions, but most did business close to home. Merchants spent a good deal of time traveling, taking goods from place to place. Many shared work and financial risks with business partners. They often went into banking, lending some of their profits to other merchants or nobles who needed cash.

Merchants in today's Italy and other Mediterranean areas were different from northern European merchants—they were nobles. Like nobles in the rest of Europe, they owned lands and manor houses. They also built large houses in towns and ran big businesses. Some established great banking firms. The Italian merchant became a medieval stereotype, and the Latin phrase *Genuensis, ergo mercator* (Genoese, therefore a merchant) became a common saying.

Master craftspeople were skilled artisans who had proven themselves in the eyes of other masters by producing a "masterpiece." Masters typically had a workshop, which they ran with the help of their wives and **journeymen** and **journeywomen**. Masters also taught their crafts to **apprentices**. Masters' wives were usually trained in the same craft as their husbands, but they sometimes practiced different ones.

## Wage Earners

Below the burghers in status were the people who did not own their own shops. Journeymen and journeywomen were artisans who had completed their apprenticeships but had not yet produced a masterpiece. They continued to work

▲ Fish sellers obtained their fish from merchants who brought large shipments of fish from distant places where it was plentiful. Fresh fish could only be sold in towns near a coast. Merchants took salted and smoked fish to inland towns. In winter, they also provided frozen fish.

toward this goal while working for wages for a master—often the one who had trained them. Those who did not want to stay with a certain master sometimes left town and worked for wages elsewhere. Bakers, carpenters, and many other artisans could find employment in the households of nobles.

Another group of wage earners worked directly for merchants. The merchants supplied them with raw materials, which the workers processed in their homes. The merchants then sold the finished products. Flemish wool merchants, for example, bought wool in England, which they took to workers in Flanders, who spun, wove, and dyed it. The merchants then sold the fabric all over Europe.

Some wage earners were servants who worked in shops and homes. Most burghers had servants. Servants cleaned, carried loads, and assisted artisans in the shops. In the house, they cleaned, cooked, and helped with young children. Servants usually came from poor families and began working at around age ten. Service was a way of gaining skills and meeting influential people as well as earning money.

## The Poor

There were many poor people throughout Europe. In fourteenth-century Florence, Italy, for example, more than half the population was poor. Many worked for low wages in the wool industry. Others worked as servants, peddlers, and porters. These people earned little and paid high taxes. They had no savings and owned only a few pieces of furniture. When financial problems or epidemics of disease led their employers to shut down, they were forced to sell their belongings for cash. When that money ran out, they struggled to survive.

Poor people had no representatives in town government. When they protested, asking for better working conditions or tax and debt relief, the authorities quickly stopped them by force. For example, in Florence, Italy, in 1378, the *ciompi* (poor working people) rebelled against the burghers that controlled the city. The burghers at first agreed to allow laborers to form workers' guilds, to have representatives in government, and to pay lower taxes. When the ciompi asked for their leaders to have the right to approve all laws, however, the burghers had soldiers drive off the protestors and took back control of the city.

Among the poor, there were also the sick, drifters, and the unemployed. Many of these people were beggars. They lived on the streets or under bridges. Crowds of beggars attended weddings and funerals, where the families involved distributed money to them.

Medieval people did not believe there was any way to end poverty, but they did think it was

In 1140, the Church published a book of laws calling on people to respect and help the poor. **Monasteries** and parish churches took an active part in this work. Here, a clergyman gives bread to the poor.

their duty to help the poor. The Christian Church took responsibility for looking after those who could not work. Local churches distributed meals and a little money to the needy. Wealthy people also gave money. Some left substantial amounts to the poor in their wills or sheltered poor people in their homes. Citizens' organizations gave money to the old, the sick, and widows with young children. Towns built hospitals where orphans, the sick, and the homeless found shelter. When natural disasters led to famine and widespread poverty, rulers and townspeople organized relief efforts to feed people until the next year's crop was harvested.

## Church Organization

Like medieval society as a whole, the Christian Church was also organized into levels. The head of the Church in a region was the bishop, who was a noble. His seat, or headquarters, was a cathedral in a town. The region he supervised was called a **diocese**. Dioceses were divided into parishes. Towns had many parishes, each with its own church. Each church was assigned one or more priests, who took care of the spiritual needs of their parishioners.

## Family Life

Most men and women usually married people of the same social **rank**. Among the wealthy, marriages were planned to bring the families political, economic, or social advantages. Both bride and groom brought money or other valuables to the union to start their married life.

Wealthy people drew up formal contracts spelling out what each family would contribute, such as a house, part of a business, or hundreds of gold coins. Ordinary people often worked for a few years to save money for marriage. Apprentices were rarely allowed to marry, so young artisans had to wait until they finished their training.

▶ Wealthy couples were accompanied by musicians on the way to their weddings. The priest met them outside the church. There, they said their marriage vows holding each other's right hand. The couple and their families went inside then to hear the priest say Mass. The musicians played for the couple again on the way back to the wedding feast.

Typically, men had to wait to get married until they could support a family, so most men were older than their brides. Because few people lived past the age of forty, many men died while their wives were still young. Young women often died in childbirth. Diseases, such as the plague, sometimes killed several members of a family. Spouses who survived frequently remarried.

## Merchant Households

In noble merchant families, the older men headed the family and the business, and the younger men worked for them. Grandparents, parents, aunts, uncles, and cousins lived together. Including servants, some noble merchant households numbered up to forty people. Family members who did not fit in the family home as well as distant relatives and business associates had houses on the same street.

Non-noble merchants had smaller households. Nevertheless, these households were still quite large, with children, stepchildren, apprentices, and servants. Sometimes they included tutors and business assistants. Merchants' wives ran the households and usually did not work with their husbands.

Like most medieval families, merchant families might have many children—ten or more—yet in some families, only two or three children reached adulthood. Many babies died soon after birth, so families took babies to be baptized the day they were born. Baptism made the babies part of the Christian Church and, therefore, able to go to heaven if they died right away. Most merchant families put children in the care of a **wet nurse**—at her house—for the first two years or so. After that, mothers raised their own children. Fathers who traveled did not see their children for long periods.

All children were taught to obey and respect adults. Physical punishment was common for children who did not behave. Formal studies

## Godparents

Most children had three godparents. Girls had two godmothers, and boys had two godfathers. Godparents normally gave their godchildren expensive presents and forged special ties with the family. Many parents wanted to name all the influential people they could as godparents. The Church, however, limited them to three.

▲ Artisan families spent much of their day together. A family is shown here talking in front of the fire. The mother is not simply relaxing, however. She spins thread while she enjoys time with her family.

began around age seven, either at home with tutors or at schools. Some boys were apprenticed with successful merchants, but not all boys went into business. Some went into law or the Church. These boys went to the university at age fourteen. Those who did go into business often began to travel with their fathers when they were teenagers. Marco Polo, for example, left for Asia with his father and uncle when he was about seventeen. Girls finished their schooling by age twelve. They either married in the next few years or became nuns.

## Artisan Households

Many master craftspeople had large households. Besides parents and children, the households included apprentices and servants. The master and mistress were expected to clothe, feed, and train or pay them. If a son or son-in-law had taken over the family business, the household might include three generations under one roof. Journeymen and journeywomen, however, did not live with the masters for whom they worked.

The children of artisans spent their early years with both parents because artisan fathers did not travel much. About age seven, the children began apprenticeships but rarely under their own parents. Boys were apprenticed to outside craftsmen, and girls to outside craftswomen. More often, though, girls became servants in a household. Apprentices often developed close relationships with the master's family, which substituted for their own. As members of the household, apprentices were required to do

chores and run errands. The master and mistress disciplined them when needed.

Some young women stayed home and worked in their father's shops until marriage. Unlike wealthy girls, female artisans were not forced to marry or become nuns because they could support themselves with their skills.

## APPRENTICESHIP CONTRACT

*"John Goffe has put himself to John Pentreath to learn the craft of fishing, and to stay with him as his apprentice until the end of eight years fully complete. Throughout this time, John Goffe shall well and truly serve John Pentreath and Agnes his wife. . . . And John Pentreath and Agnes his wife shall teach John Goffe the craft of fishing in the best way they know, chastising [punishing] him duly, and finding him food, clothing and shoes as befits an apprentice."*
**Records of the County of Cornwall, England, 1459** [4]

# town Government

ings and nobles owned the lands where towns arose, so people had to get their permission to settle there and carry on business. Burghers soon got organized, however, and began to run the towns themselves.

### The Charter

Burghers had different interests from those of nobles (also called lords). For example, lords regularly charged tolls to merchants traveling on their roads and rivers. Tolls could significantly cut into a merchant's profits, so merchants wanted tolls removed. Townspeople had to pay whatever taxes the lord wanted to charge, such as a poll tax (a set amount every resident was charged). Burghers wanted to get rid of the lords' tax collectors. Tax collectors earned money by overcharging townspeople and keeping the extra cash for themselves. Town dwellers wanted to pay the lord a set amount and keep any extra for the upkeep of the town. Towns also needed laws to regulate business, governments to make those laws, and courts to settle disagreements.

Burghers formed groups called **communes** to keep the public order within towns and regulate business. Little by little, communes negotiated with lords to get more rights for townspeople.

In some areas, towns became independent of lords. In twelfth-century Italy, a group of

◀ The city of Brugge (also called Bruges) in today's Belgium was under the authority of the counts of Flanders, who encouraged trade and willingly gave their towns charters. In the fourteenth century, Brugge became an international trade center with a Hanseatic League office. The bell tower rising above the houses and canal belongs to the Market Hall.

northern towns formed the Lombard League and defeated the **Holy Roman Emperor**, who controlled the region at the time. He gave them freedom to govern themselves. In the twelfth and thirteenth centuries, northern German merchants and towns organized themselves into the Hanseatic League. Members established new towns, wrote their own laws, and controlled trade around the Baltic Sea.

In most places, communes preferred to cooperate with their lords. Lords had the military might to keep the peace, so that merchants could travel safely and business could thrive. Most lords saw towns and cities as good sources of cash income from taxes and rewarded them with charters.

A charter was a written contract that detailed the rights and privileges a lord gave to a town, such as the right to collect its own taxes and the right to set up its own laws and courts. Charters typically gave people freedom from paying tolls and personal freedom to serfs who had lived in the town for one year and one day. They gave towns the right to have markets and trade fairs. In return, the commune agreed to be loyal to the lord, to pay taxes, and to either give money or serve as soldiers if the lord went to war.

In medieval society, lords owned all the property. Their free subjects rented the land they used. Serfs were allowed to use some land for themselves in exchange for their labor. Business people, however, wanted to be able to buy and sell land like any other item. Charters allowed town dwellers to own property, so they could buy and sell it.

## Government Officials

Over time, communes became town councils. Town councillors made laws and served as judges in courts. The mayor was the head of the town. He was in charge of running

### SPANISH TOWN CHARTER

*"I Alfonso [II], by the grace of God, king of Aragon . . . approve, concede and confirm . . . the ancient customs and rights of Jaca. . . .*

*First of all, I approve and confirm that the men of Jaca may dispose freely of the goods and property that God has given them. . . .*

*You may hold fairs every year during the feast of the Holy Cross. We receive all those who attend these fairs under our protection and safeguard, whosoever they may be and from wheresoever they may come."*
**Charter of Jaca, Spain, 1187** [5]

the government and making sure that laws were obeyed. He served as a judge, too.

Councillors and the mayor were usually elected by the masters of the different guilds, or they simply chose their own successors. In some towns, the lord appointed them to office. In other towns, the citizens elected them. In general, only men who had been born in the town or had lived there for a long time were considered citizens. Clergy did not take part in government and neither did nobles, unless they were engaged in business. Journeymen and other wage earners had no say in how their towns were governed.

To protect their own interests, guilds worked to get their candidates on the town council. Guilds wanted to make sure that laws were favorable to their members and their types of business. Tensions arose within the government because what was good for people in one occupation was not always good for people in others.

Town governments frequently came under the control of a small group of powerful families or even one powerful family. Thirteenth-century Venice, for example, had 480 seats on its Grand Council, but twenty-seven families held half of them. In some towns and cities, such as Florence and Mantua in today's Italy, a single family was able to take control. In others, such as Cologne (now Köln) in modern-day Germany, the guilds took control.

## Running the Government

Town governments created bureaucracies. Bureaucracies were departments and offices that took care of the day-to-day running of government. Towns hired many officials and clerks.

The officials included accountants, tax collectors, and notaries who kept written records. Some officials monitored the markets to ensure fair practices. Others were concerned with public health—making sure the food sold in markets was safe to eat, for instance. Others maintained public buildings or supervised taverns. Town watchmen kept the peace, patrolling the town walls during the day and policing the streets at night. Some officials were in charge of keeping wild swine and donkeys out of the town. Most positions were part-time, and the people who took them were also running their own businesses. In addition, all men belonged to the town militia, or army. The militia defended the town in case of attack.

## Law and Justice

The town councillors made laws that governed the way business was done. The laws spelled out what practices were fair and honest. They established fair weights and measurements for products. Some laws protected different types of businesses by limiting what each type of shop could sell. For example, in the fourteenth century, shops in London were not allowed to sell both codfish and shellfish. Some laws governed how contracts were drawn up and how a merchant could prove he had paid for goods. Other laws regulated debts and bankruptcy. Lawyers, trained at universities, worked for the government and businesses. They began to interpret laws more precisely and consistently.

Townspeople ordinarily came into contact with three types of courts: the lord's court, town

▲ The King's Bench in England was the court of the king, the highest of all lords. Groups of judges and their assistants traveled around the country and heard cases at different stops. The accused are pictured in front, chained and guarded by officers with staffs. The judges sit in the back listening, while their clerks take notes.

court, and Church court. The lord's court usually tried cases of "high justice." These cases involved violent crimes, such as robbery, assault, and murder. A noble did not personally hear these cases but had officials who did so in his place. Punishments for high crimes included hanging, branding, and flogging but seldom prison time.

Town courts heard cases involving business issues and lesser crimes, such as fraud, theft, and minor assaults. These courts also handled disagreements between neighbors and dealt with public nuisances. Town courts collected fines, handed out punishments like the **pillory**, and confiscated illegal goods, such as underweight loaves of bread.

Church courts handled cases involving marriage, wills, and heresy (violations of Church law). In most towns, the lord's court was the court of appeals. In the thirteenth century, cities began to establish their own courts of appeal, such as the *Parlement de Paris*.

## Women's Rights

Compared to men, women had few legal and political rights. Single women and widows could own property, manage their own businesses, and sign contracts. Married women were not allowed to handle these legal matters alone. Married women had to get their husbands' consent to go to court, although they had some legal rights. All women had to pay taxes on their own or through their husbands. In general, however, they could not serve as witnesses in court, vote in elections, or hold political office. In fact, they could not even attend political meetings.

## Paying Taxes

Towns collected taxes to pay their lords and for their own upkeep. Money was needed for maintaining the town wall, the town hall, and the cathedral, and all town employees had to be paid.

Outsiders paid a tax for the privilege of doing business in a town. Part of the money went to the town and part to the lord. The basic tax paid by residents was a property tax. The amount each person owed in taxes was based on how much property he or she owned. The tax rates were often tipped in favor of the wealthy

burghers who made the laws, however. In Troyes, in today's France, for example, those with the most property did not have to tell the government how much property they had but could simply pay a flat tax that was a small part of their income. On the other hand, ordinary people had to say how much they owned and paid a greater portion of their incomes. Sometimes, poor wage earners had to sell their possessions to pay their taxes. If they did not pay their taxes, they were put in jail. People also paid sales taxes and poll taxes. Since towns were devoted to buying and selling, sales taxes brought in considerable income.

Lords sometimes charged additional taxes. Lords charged them to pay off high debts or to go on a Crusade. Townspeople resisted paying these taxes, but they could not completely refuse. In part because burghers were unwilling to pay, the number of nobles who went on Crusades decreased over time.

▶ Town officials are seen collecting taxes from merchants in fifteenth-century Paris. Towns kept records of what people owed and who had paid. Only people who were extremely poor were excused from paying taxes.

# CHAPTER 4

# Working Life

**D**uring the twelfth and thirteenth centuries, the **money economy** developed; that is, people paid for products with money rather than trading goods with one another. International trade grew. Merchants and artisans organized themselves into guilds to protect their business interests.

## The Money Economy

The money economy affected everyone. Nobles and peasants who lived in the country bought items in town that could not be made at home. They also sold farm products in town. Peasants sold their extra eggs, cheeses, and produce at street stalls. Nobles sold their raw wool to local merchants.

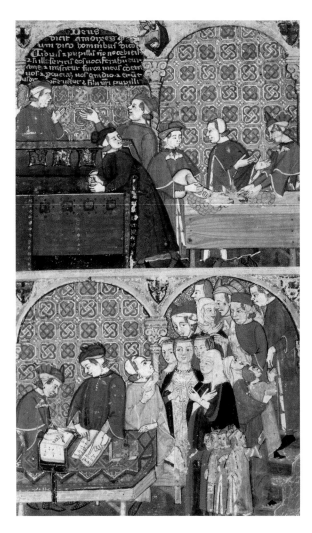

An important part of the money economy was banking. Banking included moneylending. To pay for a war or build a new church, nobles and bishops often preferred taking out loans to selling some lands or gold objects. Merchants charged very high interest rates for lending money, but they ran the risk that a borrower might refuse to pay back a loan.

Ordinary people sometimes needed help to survive. Merchants loaned money to peasants who needed it to live on until the next harvest. Shopkeepers let good customers buy on credit. Men and women with extra money also made small loans, with interest, to neighbors.

Other types of banking were meant for business. Banks made large loans to merchants and invested money in industry and shipbuilding. People deposited money in banks to get interest on it. Banks made money by lending those deposits at higher interest rates than they paid. Christian merchants began to use checks, which Arab and Jewish merchants had first used in Muslim lands.

Some merchants were strictly bankers. In many places, Jews became moneylenders because laws prevented them from owning farmland or

◄ The money economy was an important part of town life. This fourteenth-century book illustration shows work at a banking house. Some bankers count coins while another stores a pouch of money in a chest. Another group talks with customers and keeps records. The crowd of men and women waiting shows that people had become used to handling money.

◀ Many moneylenders held on to valuable items belonging to borrowers until borrowers paid back their loans. If a borrower did not pay back a loan, the moneylender sold the item to get his money back. A moneylender and his wife are shown here with many valuable items. These include books, gold and silver objects, and a mirror.

# Money Changing

Kings and nobles minted their own coins, and merchants had to figure out how much goods were worth in each different type of money. Money changers were people who exchanged the money a buyer had to pay for goods for another type of coin that was more useful to the seller. Money changers were experts at determining the value of coins. Values were based on how much gold and silver a coin actually contained. Merchants could not accept coins on appearance alone because lords often added a greater amount of cheap metals to coins to save on precious metals.

going into other occupations. Christians were forbidden by the Church to charge high interest rates, so Jews were often pressured to give credit to merchants and lords. Many Christians ignored this rule, however.

Other merchants were part-time bankers. They also invested money in deals that were too expensive for one merchant alone. For example, several merchants would pool their money to build ships. They made a profit when the ships were used to carry goods long distances. Other merchants invested in land and town properties.

## Occupations of Men and Women

Some merchants were **retailers**—they sold products in their own shops. The items they sold were not made by town artisans but were brought in from a distance, such as **damask** cloth from Damascus (in today's Syria) and spices from the East Indies. Retailers specialized in one type of merchandise and had goods shipped to them.

Other merchants were **wholesalers**. They purchased shiploads of goods that they sold to retailers. For example, Venetian wholesalers sold salt, timber, and grain to merchants in Constantinople (now Istanbul in Turkey). They returned from Constantinople with shiploads of spices and other luxury products that they sold in western Europe. Hanseatic-League merchants sold furs, honey, and metals in western Europe and returned to the Baltic region with wool cloth and other manufactured goods. They also bought raw products and had workers process them for

▲ Customers bought fabrics and asked tailors to make the clothes they wanted. Here, a tailor is shown looking over some fabric with a customer. The increase in trade and the Crusades familiarized Europeans with new fabrics and clothing styles from Asia. Tastes in clothes began to change, and tailors did a brisk business keeping wealthy people clothed in the latest styles.

## SILK SPINNING LAW

*"No **spinster** on large spindles may have more than three apprentices, unless they be her own or her husband's children . . . nor may she contract with them for less than 20 Parisian sols to be paid to her, their mistress. . . . No man of this craft who is without a wife may have more than one apprentice . . . if, however, both husband and wife practice the craft, they may have two apprentices and as many journeymen as they wish."*
**Thirteenth-century Paris regulation** [6]

which was more affordable than gold. In some towns, certain crafts—such as bronze casting in York, England—were reserved only for men. Other crafts—such as making silk handkerchiefs and headdresses in Paris—were only for women. Master artisans, however, were more than creators. They were involved in every aspect of commerce. They bought raw materials, hired employees, and sold products in their shops.

People provided services in a number of fields. Among them were innkeepers, barbers, and menders of clothes, furniture, and other breakable household items. Some people were

sale. They bought salt, herring, and cod in Baltic areas and sold salted fish in other parts of Europe.

Written accounts do not credit the wives of merchants with helping their husbands at work, yet many of these women understood business. It was common for widows to continue running their husbands' businesses after their deaths. Some rich widows invested in land and trade.

Male and female artisans practiced many of the same crafts, including tailoring, glove making, wood turning, bookbinding, butchering, and brewing. Goldsmiths were the aristocrats of artisans. They used expensive materials, and their work was painstaking and slow. Most of the pieces they sold were actually made of silver,

## MARGERY KEMPE

Margery Kempe was the daughter of the mayor of Lynn, England. She was born around 1373 into a life of privilege. Although she married a wealthy burgher in 1393, her married life was not elegant enough for her. Unlike most women who worked to help support their families, Kempe worked to have more money for clothes and luxuries. She opened a brewing business, which did well for only three or four years. She then became a mill owner but had to give up that business, too. Kempe became convinced that her businesses failed because God wanted her to live a spiritual life.
So she changed course and went on several long **pilgrimages**.

peddlers. They did not make products themselves but sold anything they could buy and resell, such as candles, herbs, butter, ale, and fish—generally items used on a daily basis. Many women combined several occupations. For example, they may have been part-time spinsters, brewers, and peddlers.

## Guilds

Originally, guilds were community and religious groups. They developed into organizations for people in the same trade. People who practiced a given occupation generally lived in the same neighborhood. Guilds added to their sense of community and neighborhood pride. Guilds competed to build the most beautiful parish church in town. Some guilds built special churches and halls for their meetings and celebrations.

Merchants formed guilds for many trades— for the spice, wool, and silk businesses, and even for banking. Merchant guilds tended to be the wealthiest and most powerful guilds. Artisans formed guilds for almost all crafts, such as dyeing, parchment making, and goldsmithing. People in other occupations—porters, ostlers (people who cared for mules and horses), and boatmen—had guilds as well. Many guilds did not allow journeymen to join so that masters could keep control of the industry.

Guilds regulated their trade and protected their members. Craft guilds determined methods of production and set standards of quality. They established production quotas (the number of products each artisan should make). They decided the terms for apprenticeships—such as the number of years needed to learn a craft. Guilds inspected masters' shops to check on the quality of products and on the working conditions of apprentices and journeymen. Guilds also set prices for their products. Merchant guilds helped

▼ In this picture, members of the guild of fish sellers in Venice meet in their hall. Guild halls were not just used for business meetings. They also served as social clubs. Guild members took pride in their halls. The fish sellers paid for fancy woodwork for their ceiling.

members share risks. For instance, groups of merchants sometimes hired several ships, and each merchant sent only a portion of his merchandise in each ship. That way, if one ship were sunk or robbed, the loss of merchandise would not ruin any of the merchants. Finally, guilds paid for members' funerals and maintained a fund for their widows and orphans.

Guilds also performed many civic duties. They purchased fire buckets and ladders, and members served as firefighters. They financed schools, hospitals, orphanages, and charitable activities. Guilds sponsored festivals—typically for their patron (protector) **saints**—which featured plays and other public entertainment.

By and large, craftswomen could join guilds and become masters in many fields. Guild rules

▼ The seated man dressed in fine clothes is a master craftsman. He is checking the work of a stonemason, who is cutting a piece of stone for a building. The man on the right is a carpenter. Masters checked the work of apprentices and journeymen to see if it was skillful enough for them to become masters.

## GUILD ORDINANCES

*"[The leather workers] have ordained that they will find a wax candle, to burn before Our Lady in the church of All Hallows near London Wall. Also that each person of the said trade shall put in the box such sum as he shall think fit, in aid of maintaining the said candle. . . .*

*And if any one of the said trade shall have work in his house that he cannot complete, or if for want of assistance such work shall be in danger of being lost, those of the said trade shall aid him, so that the said work be not lost."*
**Leather workers' ordinances, London, 1346** [7]

limited women's participation, however. Craftswomen were paid less than men for the same work. They could not hold offices in most guilds or even vote for the officers. Women were usually allowed to participate in only some guild events.

Over time, problems arose for the guilds. Some larger and richer guilds tried to take over smaller, poorer ones. Masters tried to amass profits by cutting journeymen's salaries and limiting the number of people who could go into a craft. Between 1347 and 1348, the Black Death, or plague, struck; it eventually killed about 40 to 50 percent of the population of Europe. The decline in population resulted in a tremendous shortage of workers. Survivors began to demand higher wages. At first their demands were denied, but by the end of the century, wage workers succeeded in getting better pay.

### Markets and Fairs

Towns generally had a weekly market day when people from the surrounding area came to buy and sell along with the townspeople. In the market, people shopped for food and other frequently used items.

Fairs were different from markets. Fairs were held once a year for several days or even weeks. They usually took place during a religious

◄ A shoemaker, a goldsmith, and a fabric merchant are shown with their products at a fair in France. Fair officials set up tents and stalls for merchants to store their goods and do business.

holiday, such as the feast of the town's patron saint. Celebrations as well as business were among the attractions. Merchants came from a wide area, and they arranged large wholesale deals, often for expensive products, such as furs and spices. The lords of towns where fairs were held made considerable amounts of money from the taxes on these deals. Since the same merchants attended many of the same fairs, they often worked out large loans and other major financial deals at one fair and then settled them at a later one.

Merchants who acquired new products created new markets. Woolens and cotton cloth from Flanders, France, and Italy and wines from Germany and the Mediterranean region became popular in other places. Spices and sugar from Asia and the Middle East became commonplace in Europe.

The largest fairs brought together merchants from different parts of Europe. Fairs encouraged the use of standard weights, measurements, and money, which made trade easier. Merchants opened new routes as they traveled to markets and fairs, adding to the business of towns along the way. Laws for doing business used in older

markets and fairs spread as merchants moved into new markets and fairs.

Trade also promoted the development and greater use of technology. Using water mills to grind grain was common in the eleventh century. By the twelfth century, sawmills and fulling mills (where new cloth was cleaned and shrunk before dyeing) also used water power. Similarly, although rough wool cloth could be manufactured on small home looms, bigger and better looms were needed for the large panels of high-quality fabric that were sold commercially.

## Champagne fairs

The six fairs held each year in the Champagne region of France were the biggest in Europe. The count of Champagne guaranteed protection to merchants and their merchandise. The keepers of the fairs organized the fairs and used huge staffs to make sure they ran smoothly. Besides sergeants who patrolled the fair grounds and roads, there were clerks, couriers, and porters. Notaries kept records of all transactions, and tax collectors made sure the count got his fees.

# CHAPTER 5

# Education

The creation of new, well-paid jobs for educated men convinced burghers and many lesser nobles to send their sons to school. Learning to read, write, and do some mathematics would certainly help any young person interested in entering a trade. Different kinds of schools were established, and the first European universities were founded. Even the daughters of burghers might receive a basic education.

## New Need for Literacy

As kings and powerful nobles gained greater control of their lands in the eleventh and twelfth centuries, they hired educated men to help run their governments. They needed officials to interpret laws, write documents, and keep accurate records. Cities and towns also needed educated officials. Merchants needed employees who could speak foreign languages and draw up contracts. Craftspeople needed education to keep records and accounts.

## Schools

Poor children did not attend school in the Middle Ages. Families that could afford to educate their children hired tutors or sent them to school.

Early medieval schools were run by monks in monasteries and by priests in cathedrals. Monastery schools prepared students for a religious life. Cathedral schools trained future priests but also took in the children of business people. Bishops also licensed teachers, some of whom opened private schools. Cathedral and private elementary schools had both male and female teachers. These schools taught boys and girls to read religious poems called psalms and to sing the Church **liturgy**.

After the first few years at a cathedral school, boys moved on to the secondary level. There, they studied the Latin language and Latin grammar. Composition and literature were part

◀ Teachers read aloud the books the class was studying. Schoolchildren had to be good listeners and remember what their teachers said. Often, only one copy of a book was available for the whole class, so students could not take it home to study.

of grammar. Each day, students memorized new passages from the books their teachers read to them. They had to learn Latin because their other subjects were taught in Latin. Boys studied the seven liberal arts: grammar, **rhetoric**, logic, arithmetic, geometry, astronomy, and music theory. In logic class, students were not just asked to think about problems but had to examine philosophical and theological works. Logic was considered the most important subject because medieval thinkers believed that, through logical thinking, it was possible to answer all questions, including those about faith and God.

Some cathedral schools taught **theology**, law, medicine, or literature to very advanced students. Various schools became famous, and some masters, or teachers, became so well known that they attracted students from all over Europe. One of these masters was Peter Abelard, who taught in Paris during the twelfth century. Abelard examined how changes in the meaning of words over time created confusion. In his textbook *Sic et Non* (Yes and No), Abelard presented moral and philosophical contradictions followed by quotations from Church authorities on both sides. His challenging and stimulating teaching drew crowds of students.

In the eleventh and twelfth centuries, merchants and artisans began establishing town schools to give their children a more practical education for business. Their children could now go to cathedral schools, town schools, or schools run by nuns. In town elementary schools, children learned prayers, the fundamentals of religion, good manners, and to read the **vernacular** (their native language). Some schools taught Latin. After a few years, boys went into an apprenticeship or moved to more advanced schools that emphasized arithmetic for business or Latin and the liberal arts. Afterward, boys could continue their studies at a university.

Girls stayed in elementary school until age twelve or so, studying reading, embroidery, and music.

## Wandering Scholars

Some students traveled around Europe, stopping in as many schools as they could to study under famous masters. These students came to be known as wandering scholars. The songs of the wandering scholars describe a life of eating, drinking, and having fun, and the students developed a reputation for living irresponsibly. Still, many wandering scholars became respected Church and government officials.

## Apprenticeships

Artisan parents apprenticed their children to other masters, who agreed to teach the children a craft or skill. A contract was prepared, and parents paid the master's guild to guarantee that the child would complete the apprenticeship. Parents often paid the master a second fee for the child's living expenses.

Masters were expected to give apprentices a well-rounded education. The children were taught good manners and religion as well as reading, writing, and arithmetic. Apprentices spent most of their time learning their crafts, though. Masters demonstrated and explained tasks, and then the apprentices practiced. Apprentices worked long days—from dawn to dusk—alongside their masters.

The length of an apprenticeship depended on the craft. Weaving could be learned in four or five years. Goldsmithing required ten years. At the end of that period, a board of masters from the guild examined the apprentice. If the apprentice produced a masterpiece, he or she became a master. Usually, apprentices were promoted to

◀ The University of Salamanca, Spain, was founded in 1218. Students there could study religious law, the Latin language and literature, the liberal arts, or physics. The building in the rear with the coat of arms was built in the fifteenth century. It had large classrooms with rough wooden benches for the students.

journeymen. Masters typically gave a set of tools, new clothes, and some money to new journeymen. The guild board examined journeymen again some years later to see if they qualified as masters.

## Universities

During the twelfth century, cathedral schools developed into universities. The professors and students formed guilds. In Latin, the word *universitas* means "guild." University guilds regulated many aspects of teaching and student life, from the curriculum and course fees to the price of lodging and materials.

Many medieval professors were scholastics. The scholastics were scholars who tried to show that faith and reason did not contradict each other. They studied the works of ancient Greek and medieval Islamic philosophers. They raised questions about theology, nature, law, and philosophy and, like Peter Abelard, examined opposing points of view. The scholastics then tried to arrive at a correct answer. They compiled questions about subjects in books called *summas*.

Universities had specialties. The university in Bologna, Italy, focused on law. The universities in Salerno, Italy, and Montpellier, France, taught medicine. The university in Paris specialized in theology and logic. Over time, numerous universities were established in Europe with the support of rulers, nobles, and the Christian Church.

Only males studied at universities. Most were teenagers, living completely on their own. They had to make their own living arrangements and get professors to accept them into their classes. Colleges with residence halls were established in some universities by the fifteenth century.

University students first had to finish studying the liberal arts (grammar, rhetoric, logic,

## AN EXPENSIVE LIFE

*"This is to inform you that I am studying at Oxford with the greatest diligence, but the matter of money stands greatly in the way of my promotion as it is now two months since I spent the last of what you sent me. The city is expensive and makes many demands; I have to rent lodgings, buy necessaries, and provide for many other things which I cannot now specify. Wherefore I respectfully beg your paternity that by the promptings of divine pity you may assist me, so that I may be able to complete what I have well begun."*
**Letter from an Oxford University student in England to his father, thirteenth century** [8]

▲ Many students already had their bachelor's degree when they went to the University of Bologna, Italy (*shown above*). Many had positions in the Church or government but felt that a law degree would be useful for their work.

arithmetic, geometry, astronomy, and music theory). Professors taught by lecturing—they read a text, explained it, presented various opinions about it, and resolved the differences in opinions. The text typically came from the Bible, the works of the Greek philosopher Aristotle, or the works of Roman writers, such as Cicero or Virgil. Students memorized the lectures and took notes. Sometimes professors raised questions and asked students for answers. The disputations (discussions) that followed gave students practice in arguing different points of view.

After about five years of studying the liberal arts, students were examined by a panel of professors. Those who passed an oral exam were awarded their bachelor's degree and licensed to teach liberal arts. Students could then study law or another field. Becoming a master took ten to fifteen years in all.

Relations between universities and towns were not always smooth. Because students were considered members of the clergy, when they got into trouble, they were tried by Church courts rather than town courts. Lords and kings gave universities special rights that made them independent communities within towns. Students often behaved badly, but towns profited from

having them. After all, students spent money on rooms and food, and a university increased a town's reputation.

## Books

In the Middle Ages, books and documents were kept in the libraries of cathedrals and monasteries. In the thirteenth century, universities began their own book collections. In 1290, the University of Paris had 1,017 books. Parish churches often had a few books that parishioners could consult. Both university libraries and churches had popular books chained so that people could not take them.

Books were expensive because they were made by hand. Stationery shops kept libraries of textbooks for students to rent and copy. Students with more money could hire professional copyists or buy books from booksellers.

Most individuals who owned books had very few. Personal collections had some books written in Latin, but many were written in the vernacular. Prayer books and books about the lives of saints were popular. People also owned romances and collections of tales. Highly educated people—such as doctors—owned Latin grammar books and works about their professions. Some people owned books on accounting, estate management, and how to write business letters.

## translations from Arabic

During the twelfth century, northern Europeans began to travel to Spain, Sicily, and the Middle East to obtain Latin translations of Greek and Arabic works. They had the ancient texts translated from Greek into Arabic and then into Latin. Many lost works of Aristotle were recovered this way. Arabic mathematical and scientific works, such as *Algebra* by the Middle Eastern mathematician al-Khawarizmi, were brought to Europe for the first time.

# CHAPTER 6

# Daily Life

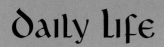

hurch bells regulated everyday life. They rang every three hours for the eight **canonical hours** (traditional times for prayer). People listened to them to know when to open and close their shops. In the fourteenth century, the hourly chimes of town clocks began ordering people's lives even more.

## Eating and Drinking

The prime bells at dawn were the signal to start the working day. Homemakers would go from the grocers' street to the poultry dealers' to the bakers' to purchase items needed for that day. Some shops sold raw products, while others sold prepared foods like bread and fish pies. Some cooked foods of the Middle Ages—flawns (cheese custards) and wafers (cookies), for instance— were fancy. Prepared foods could be bought in individual portions or in larger amounts to feed a family.

Bread was the most important food people ate. They filled up on bread and ate small amounts of other foods. Bread was made of different kinds of grain, such as wheat, barley, oats, and rye. The grains were combined to make different kinds of loaves.

Meat was expensive even though many different kinds were available. Wealthy people ate chicken, goose, duck, beef, pork, rabbit, hare, and mutton. If they lived near the coast, they ate different kinds of seafood, including oysters and eels. If they lived inland, they ate freshwater fish. Fish spoiled very quickly, so much of it was salted and dried. They also ate cheese and eggs. Recipes called for many spices and herbs. In most of Europe, fruits and vegetables were plentiful in summer but harder to come by in winter. Only dried fruits and onions, carrots, and other vegetables that kept in the cold were available off-season. Around the warm Mediterranean Sea, fresh foods were available longer.

◄ Housewives brought their loaves to a baker, who baked them for a fee. Bakers made loaves that they sold to people who could not make their own dough. The prices varied according to the kinds of grain used. Bakers also supplied inns and taverns.

This picture shows a banquet for wealthy people. Servants carry platters of food. The tables are covered with white linen tablecloths. Musicians entertain the guests from above.

Ordinary people had a much more limited diet. They ate mostly grains. They normally ate coarse, heavy bread. Sometimes they made hot cereal instead of bread. Oats, beans, and barley were the most common additions to their daily meals. In parts of southern Europe, for example, people ate rice. Wage workers could not possibly afford to eat vegetables, fish, or dairy products every day. Meat was a luxury that they ate only on special occasions.

Most people drank alcoholic beverages—wine, ale, or beer. Some clergy advised against this practice, but the water available was not always safe because rivers were often polluted. Towns had pipes that carried in water from streams and springs, but sometimes businesses used most of the water, leaving little for households.

Burgher families ate two meals a day, one in the late morning and one in the late afternoon. Everyday meals usually consisted of a stew, soup, or roast followed by fruit and nuts. The family ate first, and the apprentices and servants ate after them. Leftovers were given to beggars who knocked on the door.

Burghers gave elaborate dinners on special occasions like weddings and Christmas. They served many roasts and stews, breads scented and colored with herbs, and sweet desserts and imported fruits. Special dishes, such as boar's head or roast swan with its feathers, were paraded before the guests before carving.

Good manners were important to burghers. Manners smoothed business relations and helped establish a man's reputation at guild dinners. Medieval table manners involved more than wiping one's mouth before drinking. People shared cups and ate with their hands, so there were rules to follow when handing over a cup and specific fingers to use for eating different foods.

At meals for the wealthy, a rectangular table was covered with a cloth. The table settings were placed on one side, and the servants served from the other. Each diner had a spoon, an assortment of knives for bread, meats, and shellfish, and a trencher—a large piece of old bread that served as a plate. A cup and a two-handled bowl for soups and stews were placed between each pair of diners.

The Christian Church calendar determined what people ate during much of the year. On many days, such as Fridays and the forty days of

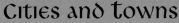 

► Guests at an inn ate, drank, and socialized with each other. Complete strangers who stayed for the night not only shared a table—they often shared a bed.

**Lent**, people were required to fast. They did not give up eating altogether, but they ate less on these days. Only one meal was served. Fish, rather than meat, was served on fast days. During Lent, the wealthy ate coarse, dark breads rather than lighter, white loaves. On feast days, such as the New Year's holiday, people ate in excess, as a reminder of all the good things God had created. In general, though, the Church advised people to eat only as much as they needed to live.

Some people used food as a symbol of power. Being able to give a banquet with lavish dishes and many guests showed that a person was rich and influential.

## UNAPPETIZING COOKSHOP

*"From many pasties hast thou [you] drained the
    blood [gravy],
And numerous Jacks of Dover hast thou sold,
That have been heated twice and twice gone cold.
Many a pilgrim has called down Christ's curse;
Your parsley stuffing made them sick or worse,
That they had eaten with your straw fed goose.
For in your shop, full many a fly is loose."*
**Geoffrey Chaucer, The Canterbury Tales** [9]

## Inns and taverns

Inns and taverns were gathering places for men and women. They served food as well as drink, and inns rented rooms to travelers. Guild members regularly got together at taverns. University students were faithful visitors. Many guilds and towns set up regulations to control public drinking and prevent disorderly behavior in taverns.

### Fashions

The Christian Church advised people to dress simply, stressing that spiritual things were what mattered, not outward show. Many people, however, wanted to wear the most beautiful and luxurious clothes they could. Wealthy burghers copied the fashions of the nobility. The rich wore clothes made of fine wool in bright colors. Their winter garments were lined or trimmed with fur. Most people could not afford fur or expensive fabrics, however.

Everyone dressed in layers. Men wore linen underwear, long tunics, and robes. In about the thirteenth century, they began wearing short tunics with breeches, stockings, tall leather boots, and belted coats. Outdoors, they wore mantles, or rounded capes. Men cut their hair just below their ears or a little longer and wore cloth hats or turbans. Some wore hoods. They shaved about once a week.

Women wore long linen chemises or slips under tunics and sleeveless gowns. Their shoes were made of leather. They kept their long hair braided and covered their heads and necks with linen veils called wimples. In the fifteenth century, wealthy women began wearing cone-shaped hats with veils and other more fanciful headdresses. Many women, against Church advice, used makeup.

Craftspeople needed practical clothes for work. They avoided wide sleeves and roomy robes that

could catch fire or get caught in their equipment. Their top layer of clothing was frequently an apron.

## Religion in Daily Life

Medieval people were religious. Most Europeans were Christians, and they went to Mass every week. Most prayed to saints, believing that saints could perform miracles and ask God to help them. All cathedrals and many churches had the **relics** of a saint. Relics were bones or pieces of the saint's belongings that people believed brought them closer to the saint. People also worshiped the consecrated **host**, or bread, at Mass. They believed it was the body of Christ and that it could grant them forgiveness and healing. The Feast of Corpus Christi (body of Christ) was one of the most important feasts of the year. During this feast, people carried the host in a procession through the town. People also worshiped the Virgin Mary. They prayed to her to intercede for them when Christ judged them after death.

Many people wanted a more intense and personal religious experience than Church services provided. In the thirteenth century, townspeople began to form confraternities. These were groups of people from different social levels and neighborhoods who got together to pray. Members helped each other with personal and economic problems and performed charitable works. They built schools and chapels in churches. Getting together to sing the liturgy and read the Bible was their most important work.

Others joined new religious orders, such as the Dominicans, who worked as teachers, and the Franciscans, who worked with the urban poor. Many townspeople joined brotherhoods and sisterhoods—single-sex groups who lived pious lives, sometimes in poverty. The Beguines, a popular sisterhood in northern European towns, was made up of women who lived together without becoming nuns. They supported themselves through their crafts—such as weaving and making lace—and by caring for the aged or sick.

▲ The clothes of the couple in the painting show that they were rich. The husband's tunic and mantle are trimmed with fur. The wife's green gown is so long and has so much fabric that she has to hold it up to walk. Her clothes are trimmed with fur too, even the hem of the blue tunic she wears underneath.

In their communities, they shared a deeply spiritual and prayerful life.

Many people flocked to hear sermons preached by friars on street corners and in marketplaces. Some townspeople went on pilgrimages to the great holy cities of Rome, Jerusalem, and Santiago de Compostela in Spain. Others made shorter trips to nearby shrines.

## Medieval Judaism

Jews were a small part of the population of Europe. They lived very similar lives to Christians. Jewish townspeople practiced the same occupations and often did business with Christian merchants.

Religion set Jews apart from Christians, however. A town's Jewish community lived in its own section and governed itself. Jewish neighborhoods originally formed because people wanted to live near their synagogues (houses of worship) and schools. Eventually, Christian officials required Jews to live in separate neighborhoods. In 1215, the Christian Church required Jews to wear clothes that made them easy to identify. Jews were also subject to the whims of the lord, who generally protected them but might drive them away to take over their property. The religious spirit that led many Christians to go on Crusades against Muslims also led to violent attacks against entire Jewish communities. Prejudice increased to the point that, in 1492, Ferdinand and Isabella, rulers of much of what is now Spain, expelled all Jews from that country.

In Islamic cities, Jews usually were treated well. Muslims respected Judaism and allowed Jews to take part in the life of their cities. Most Jewish people worked in business, but some served as government officials.

Jewish townspeople celebrated religious holidays with special services at their synagogues. Services included sermons and singing and chanting prayers. Ordinary daily services were shorter, but working people were not required to go, except on the Sabbath (from Friday at sunset to Saturday at sunset).

## Holidays

Guilds and confraternities sponsored celebrations on the feasts of their patron saints or other holy days. The town hosted celebrations in honor of its saint or when kings or great nobles visited. On these occasions, townspeople marched in processions to the church or cathedral, where Mass was celebrated. People staged religious pageants and other types of entertainment. Banquets typically followed.

Towns also commemorated important dates in their histories with special celebrations. These events often included ball games and other contests, such as wrestling matches and horse races. Townspeople wore the colors of their favorite competitors. Sometimes, powerful

◄ Jewish weavers are shown making tapestries. Jewish artisans learned the same skills as Christian artisans, but they were not allowed to join the guilds that set the standards for their trade.

# Muslim Life

Culture was an important part of life in Muslim cities. Rulers encouraged culture by gathering poets and scholars around them. Cities were alive with music and poetry. Books were written on many subjects. Some people wrote Arabic dictionaries and grammar books. Scientists wrote about medicine, agriculture, astronomy, and geography. Others put together collections of historical and literary works. Several cookbooks were written in Islamic Spain. Cities had large libraries. For wealthy people, having their own libraries became a status symbol.

Ordinary Muslim men worked as artisans and merchants. Muslim women were more separated from public life than Jewish and Christian women, however. They stayed home, caring for their children and their homes, although ordinary women went outdoors to buy food or run errands. Wealthy women usually remained home and sent out servants. When they did go out, wealthy women wore veils.

Christians were not as comfortable in Islamic Spain as Jews. Christianity was tolerated but discouraged. Many Christians converted to Islam. Others were attracted by the lively culture around them and adopted Arabic ways. When Christians took back Islamic lands in Europe, at first they allowed Muslims, Christians, and Jews to live side by side in peace. By the fifteenth century, however, they made Muslims convert to Christianity or leave their lands.

leaders personally financed public celebrations. The Italian statesman Lorenzo de' Medici, for example, spent ten thousand ducats on a joust in Florence in 1469. Towns also celebrated traditional seasonal holidays, such as May Day. On May Day in Padua, Italy, young women went into a wood and cardboard castle, which young men "attacked" using flowers as weapons.

▼ Visits by kings were special events for the entire town. Here, a crowd has gathered to watch Emperor Charles IV and the members of his court arrive at the church of Saint Denis near Paris in 1378. More people watch from upstairs windows. Many clergymen wait to welcome the emperor at the church door.

# CHAPTER 7

# Entertainment

Medieval people had to make their own fun: playing games, singing songs, and telling each other stories. Adults and children enjoyed many of the same activities, even games that seem like child's play today. Guilds staged plays and people enjoyed beautiful music played by cathedral musicians and performances by professional entertainers.

## Games and Pastimes

Children had many different pastimes. They played organized games like follow the leader and who can jump highest. Their toys included hoops, horseshoes, balls, marbles, and tops. They blew soap bubbles. They ran races and walked on stilts. Girls played with dolls, and boys formed teams and played war.

Adults and children played table games, such as chess, checkers, backgammon, and dice. Many adults liked to gamble on games. Families played

◄ Chess was a popular game that people of all ranks played. There were different versions of the game. Some involved using dice to determine the moves.

parlor games like charades or tried to make one another laugh. Storytelling was probably the most common form of entertainment, and telling riddles was popular. Outdoor games included blindman's bluff and bowling.

Popular sports for boys were wrestling, swimming, and playing team ball games. In London, when teams of schoolboys and apprentices played games against each other, it was customary for their fathers and other men to go watch. Boys also practiced archery, swordplay, and throwing the javelin. These sports were considered good activities for boys who might someday have to defend their towns.

Many burghers enjoyed hunting and hawking (hunting with birds of prey). Dancing was popular, although many clergy condemned it. Since even wealthy people worked long hours, perhaps the most popular adult pastime was just relaxing and talking with friends.

## SLIDING, SLEDDING, AND SKATING

*"When the great marsh that washes the Northern walls of the city is frozen, dense throngs of youths go forth to disport themselves upon the ice. Some gathering speed by a run, glide sidelong, with feet set well apart, over a vast space of ice. Others make themselves seats of ice like millstones and are dragged along by a number who run before them, holding hands. . . . Others there are, more skilled to sport upon the ice, who fit to their feet the shinbones of beasts, lashing them beneath their ankles, and with iron-shod poles in their hands they strike ever and anon against the ice and are borne along swift as a bird in flight."*
**William Fitzstephen, A description of London, c. 1180s** [10]

## Literature

Although some educated **laypeople** read for pleasure, most people had to listen to recitations.

*Chansons de geste*, or songs about great deeds, became very popular. These were long **epics** telling the adventures of the knights of the Holy Roman Emperor Charlemagne. People also liked epics about King Arthur's knights and the Spanish hero, El Cid. Townspeople enjoyed funny epics describing the adventures of tricksters like Renard the Fox, who satirized society and got themselves into funny scrapes. Comic poems and tales had exaggerated, stereotyped characters, such as fools, pretentious nobles without money, and priests who chased women. The stories were often harshly critical of women, presenting them as dishonest and disloyal. Many of these works ended with a moral, or lesson.

Courtly romances were long poems that told a story about the love of a knight for his lady. In general, these poems were not popular with townspeople, but the *Romance of the Rose* was an exception. Part of the poem is highly cynical and speaks poorly of society, rulers, women, and marriage. A French writer named Christine de Pisan attacked the *Romance of the Rose* and other antifemale works for their unfair criticism, starting a lively argument about the differences in the nature of men and women.

Those who knew Latin read Latin poetry, both classical and contemporary. Medieval poets, writing in Latin, often imitated the style of ancient writers. They wrote epics, love poems, and religious poems. Most of these poems were written by **clerics**.

In the thirteenth century, people began to write serious poetry in the vernacular. In Italy, Dante Alighieri and Francesco Petrarch examined questions about love, morals, politics, and religion in beautiful, expressive language. In the *Divine Comedy*, for example, Dante describes his imaginary spiritual journey through hell, purgatory, and heaven. The things he sees lead him to comment on corrupt politicians and Church leaders, romantic love, and many other

▲ In the *Divine Comedy*, Dante's guide through heaven is Beatrice, a woman he had loved in real life. At the end of his journey, she takes Dante where he can see the light of God. This illustration shows the moment when Dante sees that light and is filled with love.

subjects. These poets used complex poetic forms. Petrarch, for example, invented the sonnet. In the fifteenth century, French poet François Villon wrote ironic poems about his lost youth, being in prison, and the fear of death. He, too, was a master of poetic structure and meter.

Books narrating the lives of saints and their miracles in the vernacular were read widely. One of the most popular was Jacobus de Voragine's *Golden Legend*, which was translated into many languages from Latin. It told many saints' stories in the order of the Church calendar. Stories about Saint Francis of Assisi were also great favorites.

Clerics and lay writers began to write detailed histories in both Latin and the vernacular. They described the events of their time, interpreting them and using examples and documents to support their views. Some books were about the courts of kings, others about towns. The latter were very popular with proud citizens.

## Chaucer and Boccaccio

Two of the most successful collections of tales were *The Canterbury Tales* by Englishman Geoffrey Chaucer and *The Decameron* by Italian Giovanni Boccaccio. Both books are about a group of characters who entertain each other by telling stories.

Chaucer's characters are pilgrims on the way to the cathedral in Canterbury, England, and Boccaccio's are young people fleeing Florence, Italy, during the plague.

Through the stories and storytellers, both authors make fun of people who pretend to be upright members of the Church or good citizens but are really greedy or immoral.

## Music

Music was a traditional part of the Christian Church liturgy. Sections of the Bible were set to music and sung during Mass. Prayers and lessons tended to be simple chants, but songs of praise and thanksgiving had more elaborate melodies. Many cathedrals had highly trained musicians and choirs who performed liturgical music. They performed complex polyphonic pieces (compositions with several intertwining melodies). Originally, such works were sung only on holidays, but they became popular with clergy and worshipers alike and began to be performed more often. Laypeople also formed confraternities dedicated to performing religious music. Ordinary churchgoers sang simple songs and chants of praise and repentance. These chants were also used in holiday processions.

In the thirteenth century, cathedral musicians developed the motet, a new kind of polyphonic music. They combined a religious chant in Latin with melodies about everyday subjects in the vernacular. Motets were the first complex pieces of music that were not strictly religious. A way of writing music was also developed that showed the rhythm of the music as well as how high or low the notes were. This new way of writing notes made it easier to write and perform motets and other difficult compositions.

Townspeople enjoyed different kinds of popular music. Medieval dance music was lively and rhythmic. The songs of the wandering scholars, sung in Latin, touched on love, politics, drinking, famine, and war. In the thirteenth century, the songs of French poet-musicians called troubadours became popular. Troubadours sang in the vernacular about the love of knights for ladies. Their songs were simple—just a melody with a refrain. Troubadours accompanied themselves with a single instrument, such as a lute. Ballads, songs that told stories about heroes, such as Robin Hood, or about common folks, were also well liked by working people. Ballads were based on actual events, and many had spooky, supernatural elements.

▼ Burghers hired musicians to play at parties. Towns hired them to give public concerts and play at holiday celebrations. These musicians are playing (*from left to right*) a pipe and tabor (drum), a harp, and a lute.

## Frauenlob

Born around 1260 in Germany, Heinrich von Meissen was the first Meistersinger. He began his career as a *minnesinger*, a German troubadour. He won his first troubadour contest at age thirteen and earned his nickname, Frauenlob ("praiser of ladies"), by winning another such contest. Frauenlob earned his living as a traveling entertainer for most of his life. In about 1312, he settled in Mainz, Germany, where he opened a school for Meistersingers. His songs served as a model for later Meistersinger music. These songs combined word play with philosophical ideas and religious images. Frauenlob died in 1318.

Medieval musicians played different types of instruments. Stringed instruments included the harp and the *vielle*, a violinlike instrument that was played like a cello. Wind instruments included recorders, reedy-sounding **shawms**, and bagpipes. Percussion instruments included various types of drums and bells. Musicians played portable and table organs, too. Some instruments like the lute and the shawm were brought from Islamic Spain and the Middle East to Christian lands.

In Germany, burghers with an interest in music formed guilds called song schools. These singers came from the troubadour tradition and from the confraternities that sang religious music. Their songs were religious, and the singers performed without accompaniment. Song schools taught music and held singing competitions in their local churches. Competition winners were called Meistersingers, or master singers.

### Public Entertainment

Many medieval people liked violent spectator sports. Cockfights were popular, and some men owned their own fighting cocks. People also liked to watch animal baiting—battles between dogs and a boar, bear, or bull.

Many professional entertainers performed at fairs, markets, and castles. They worked in the towns along pilgrimage routes as well. People gathered to watch acrobats, dancers, jugglers, and animal trainers with monkeys and bears. Jongleurs were the most complete entertainers. These men and women performed alone or in groups. In addition to singing, dancing, and juggling, they recited poems and told funny and bawdy tales. They sang love songs, folk songs, chansons de geste, and other long epics about the Trojan War or Alexander the Great.

### Theater

Drama grew out of the Latin Church service. In the tenth century, when it came time to read the Easter story during Mass, different priests began reading the words of different people in the story. Similar dramatic readings were performed at Christmas. Little by little, all of Jesus' life was dramatized. Then other Biblical stories, such as the tale of Jonah and the whale, also became plays. Over time, costumes, props, hymns, and songs were added. The scenes were acted rather than just read. More and more scenes were added, and the presentation was then separated from the Mass and performed outside at the church door.

Eventually, guilds and confraternities took over the performance of these plays, which were then called mystery plays. Presentations moved from the church to a town square, and laypeople, not clerics, performed the parts. Latin was dropped, and the plays began to be performed in the vernacular. Groups of related plays were performed in cycles that sometimes took several days to complete. A cycle might begin with the story of Adam and Eve and end with Judgment Day. Laypeople made the productions more elaborate, building stages with trapdoors and mechanical equipment to create special effects. They also added social criticism and comic bits that had nothing to do with the original plays. In time, the Church separated itself from the performances.

A second type of church drama was the miracle play. Miracle plays were based on the lives and miracles of the saints and were performed on the saints' feast days.

Morality plays were staged by semiprofessional actors and became popular in the fifteenth century. The plots pitted virtues against vices in the struggle for a person's soul. Most of the characters were ideas represented in human form. The main character, typically named something like Humanity, was set upon by characters, such as Greed or Evil. Humanity was tempted by them but in the end saw his mistakes and was saved with the aid of other characters, such as Repentance and Mercy. Morality plays were quite short, with comic bits that were directly related to the plots.

Medieval people worked hard and took their religious lives very seriously. On the other hand, they appreciated the good things they had and knew how to have fun, too.

## EVERYMAN SPEAKS WITH DEATH

*EVERYMAN:*
*"Where shall I flee*
*That I might escape this endless sorrow [hell]?*
*Now, gentle Death, spare me till tomorrow,*
*That I may improve myself. . . ."*

*DEATH:*
*"No, I will not consent to that*
*Nor any man will I put off, . . .*
*See that you make yourself ready shortly,*
*For you may say this is the day*
*That no man living may escape."*
**Adapted by author, *Everyman*, a morality play, c. 1485** [11]

▼ This fifteenth-century illustration shows a performance of a miracle play about Saint Apollonia, a third-century A.D. Egyptian martyr. Townspeople are seen acting out how pagans tortured the saint by breaking all her teeth to make her give up Christianity.

**711**
Arabs begin the conquest of Spain.

**827**
Arabs capture most of Sicily.

**c. 1000**
The first towns obtain the right to set up courts (in England).

**c. 1050**
Burghers begin to establish town schools.

**1061**
Northern Europeans drive Muslim rulers out of Sicily.

**1085**
Christians capture Toledo, beginning the reconquest of southern Spain from its Muslim rulers. Christians settle in border towns.

**c. 1090**
Towns in Italy begin to demand self-government.

**1095**
Pope Urban II pleads for Crusades to the Holy Land.

**1096-1099**
First Crusade calls nobles to fight Muslims in the Holy Land. Towns are taxed to help pay for their expenses.

**c. 1100**
Runaway serfs begin to be given freedom after living one year and one day in a town.

**c. 1100**
*The Song of Roland*, the first *chanson de geste*, is written.

**c. 1122**
Peter Abelard writes *Sic et Non*.

**c. 1125**
The medical school at Salerno attracts students from other countries.

**1140**
Church publishes a book calling on Christians to help the poor.

**1147-1149**
European nobles undertake the Second Crusade to the Holy Land.

**c. 1150**
The Champagne Fairs flourish in Champagne, France.

**1158**
The Holy Roman Emperor charters the University of Bologna in Italy.

**1167**
The Lombard League is organized.

**1170**
The University of Paris is founded.

**c. 1170**
Oxford University is established.

**c. 1175**
Lay sisterhoods called Beguines are formed in Liège, Belgium, and spread through northern Europe.

**1209**
The Franciscan order is founded.

**1215**
The Dominican order is founded.

**1222**
Paris charter orders that the streets of the city be widened.

**c. 1250**
The *Parlement* of Paris functions as a court of appeals.

**c. 1260**
Jacobus de Voragine writes *The Golden Legend*.

**1265**
The Hanseatic League is formally established.

## 1310-1314
Dante writes the *Divine Comedy*.

## 1312
Frauenlob opens the first school for Meistersingers.

## c. 1335
Petrarch is actively writing sonnets.

## 1347-1353
The Black Death kills about 40 percent of the population of Europe, creating a shortage of workers.

## 1348-1353
Giovanni Boccaccio writes *The Decameron*.

## 1378
Working people, or *ciompi*, revolt against the government of Florence.

## 1380s-1390s
Geoffrey Chaucer writes *The Canterbury Tales*.

## 1397
Richard Whittington becomes lord mayor of London for the first time.

## 1399
Christine de Pisan defends women in her book *Letter to the God of Loves*.

## c. 1450
François Villon writes serious poetry in French.

## c. 1450
The printing press is developed.

## 1492
Ferdinand and Isabella conquer Granada, the last Muslim city in Spain. They expel all Jews from Spain and take over their property.

**Source References:**

[1] C. Warren Hollister, *Medieval Europe: A Short History*, Wiley, 1964, p. 1

[2] William Fitzstephen, "A Description of the Most Noble City of London," in *Those Who Worked: An Anthology of Medieval Sources*, Peter Speed (ed.), Italica Press, 1997, p. 65

[3] The Goodman of Paris, *Treatise on Morals and Home Economics*, 1392. Quoted in Eileen Power, "The Menagier's Wife," in *Medieval People*, Doubleday, 1924, p. 100

[4] Records of the County of Cornwall, 1459, Peter Speed (ed.), *see above*, p. 83

[5] Charter of Jaca, Spain, 1187. Damaso Sangorrín, "El Libro de la Cadena del Consejo de Jaca," Peter Speed (ed.), *see above*, p. 122

[6] Thirteenth-century Paris regulation. Quoted in John P. McKay, Bennett D. Hill, John Buckler, *A History of Western Society*, Houghton Mifflin, 1999, p. 353

[7] Leather workers' ordinances, London, 1346. "London Letter Book F, fol. 126," Peter Speed (ed.), *see above*, p. 84

[8] Letter from an Oxford University student to his father, thirteenth century. Quoted in Austin Lane Poole, *From Domesday Book to Magna Carta: 1087-1216*, 2nd ed., Oxford: Clarendon Press, 1955, p. 241

[9] Geoffrey Chaucer, *The Canterbury Tales: The Cook's Prologue* modernized excerpt, Peter Speed (ed.), *see above*, p. 174

[10] William Fitzstephen, "A Description of the Most Noble City of London," *see above*, p. 189

[11] *Everyman* in *The Norton Anthology of English Literature*, Vol. 1, M. H. Abrams, et al., (eds.) W. W. Norton, 1968, p. 318

**apprentices**  People who study with a master to learn a skill or craft

**artisans**  Craftspeople who made objects, such as tapestries or stained-glass windows

**barbarians**  An ancient Greek word used by Romans and later Europeans to describe foreigners. It suggests that foreigners are wild, brutal, and savage.

**bishop**  The head of the Christian Church in a region. He supervised the priests and nuns in his diocese.

**burghers**  Prosperous merchants or masters in a medieval town

**canonical hours**  Eight times during the day when priests and devout laypeople said prayers. They were spaced at three-hour intervals. The canonical hours were matins (before dawn), lauds, prime (sunrise), terce, sext, none, vespers (late afternoon), and compline (after dark).

**caravans**  Travelers who group together to help each other, usually in a hostile region, such as a desert

**clerics**  Members of the clergy, such as deacons, priests, or rabbis

**communes**  Groups of burghers formed to run towns. Communes collected taxes, kept the public order, built city walls, and regulated business. Communes also negotiated with lords to get rights established in charters.

**Crusades**  Wars Christians fought against Muslims, pagans, or heretics

**damask**  A strong, shiny fabric with designs woven into it

**diocese**  All the parishes that are under a bishop's authority

**epics**  Long poems describing the adventures of a hero

**guild**  An organization of people in the same line of work. Guilds determined work methods, standards of quality, and guidelines for training apprentices.

**Holy Roman Emperor**  Ruler of a large area of Europe in the Middle Ages that included present-day Germany, Switzerland, and northern Italy. Otto I was crowned first emperor in 962.

**host**  The consecrated bread used in the Mass

**journeymen/journeywomen**  Skilled workers who had not yet become masters

**knight**  Title given to a nobleman when he completed his military training. A knight was expected to fight for his lord in battle and to follow a military code of honor. He was called "Sir."

**laypeople**  Individuals who are not members of the clergy but who follow a religious faith

**Lent**  The forty days before Easter. It is a period of fasting and praying for the forgiveness of sins.

**liturgy**  The rites and rituals that make up a religious service

**manor**  The house and surrounding property of a noble, including the fields, woods, and village where peasants and serfs lived

**medieval**  A word that relates to and describes the Middle Ages

**monasteries**  Communities where monks or nuns lived according to a set of rules

**money economy**  A system of buying and selling goods that is based on money, not barter

**nobles**  Members of the nobility, the highest social rank in medieval society. Many nobles had titles, such as count or countess, baron or baroness.

**pagan**  A term used by Christians to refer to the religions of the Roman and Germanic people who worshiped many gods

**parchment**  An animal skin, usually sheepskin, that was prepared for use as a writing surface or in windows

**parliaments**  Conferences to discuss public affairs or the organization of political groups to form a government

**pilgrimages**  Journeys to holy places

**pillory**  A wooden board with holes for the head and hands placed in a public spot. People who committed minor crimes were often placed in one as punishment.

**rank**  A person's status or position within a community or society

**relics**  The human remains or belongings of a saint

**retailers**  People who sell goods directly to the public

**rhetoric**  Effective speaking and writing skills; one of the seven liberal arts studied during the Middle Ages

**Roman Empire**  The people and lands that belonged to ancient Rome, consisting of most of southern Europe and northern Africa from Britain to the Middle East

**saints**  People who have lived a holy life and are believed to be close to God in heaven. The Roman Catholic Church deems individuals as saints.

**serfs**  Peasants who lived on a manor and could not leave the land. Serfs were required to work on a lord's farm. In return, the lord provided protection to serfs.

**shawms**  Medieval woodwind instruments that sounded like an oboe

**spinsters**  Women who spun thread

**theology**  The study of God and religious beliefs

**vernacular**  A language or dialect native to a region

**wet nurse**  A woman who breast-fed and cared for a child that was not her own

**wholesalers**  People who sell products to other merchants

# Further Information

## Books:

Gies, Frances, and Joseph Gies. *Daily Life in Medieval Times*. New York: Black Dog & Leventhal Publishers, 1999.

Grant, Neil. *Everyday Life in Medieval Europe* (Uncovering the Story). North Mankato, MN: Smart Apple Media, 2003.

Hanawalt, Barbara A. *The Middle Ages: An Illustrated History* (Oxford Illustrated Histories). New York: Oxford University Press, 1998.

Hinds, Kathryn. *The City*. New York: Benchmark Books, 2001.

Swabey, Ffiona. *Medieval Gentlewoman: Life in a Gentry Household in the Later Middle Ages*. New York: Routledge and Kegan Paul, 1999.

## Web Sites:

### Internet Resources (The Stagg Internet Resource Site)

www.d230.org/stagg/LiskaLinks

*This is a portal to many different sites. Click on "World History" to reach links listed by topic. Try "General Topics" and "Middle Ages."*

### KidsClick! (Web search for kids by librarians)

kidsclick.org

*This portal site contains links to many different subjects. Click on "Geography/History/Biography" and then on "World History." You will find many different subjects there. Click on "Middle Ages" to find many links about life and events in this period.*

### Paris at the Time of Philippe Auguste

www.philippe-auguste.com/uk/index.html

*This web site describes Paris around 1200, including the physical environment, everyday life, work, and the university.*

### Trade Products in Early Modern History (The James Ford Bell Library)

www.bell.lib.umn.edu/Products/menu.html

*Look for the history of the trade of different products, such as cinnamon, cloves, and wool.*

### Vatican Exhibit (Library of Congress Vatican Exhibit)

www.ibiblio.org/expo/vatican.exhibit/Vatican.exhibit.html

*This site describes the growth of the Vatican Library in the late Middle Ages. It shows samples of maps and books on many subjects, from medicine to mathematics to music.*

**Disclaimer:** The web site addresses (URLs) included in this book were valid at the time of going to press. However, because of the nature of the Internet, it is possible that some addresses may have changed, or sites may have changed or been closed down since publication. While the author and publisher regret any inconvenience that this may cause readers, no responsibility for any such changes can be accepted by either the author or publisher.

## Videos/DVDs

*Just the Facts: The Middle Ages*. Goldhil Home Media, 2001. (VHS)

*Life in the Middle Ages: The Merchant*. Schlessinger Media, 2002. (VHS)

*The Middle Ages*. Tape 2, Part 4, "The Town." Tape 3, Part 5, "The Traders." Films Incorporated, 1993. (VHS)